POSTP~~ARTUM~~
~~DESPAIR~~ *happiness*

WHAT TO DO WHEN YOU **LOVE** THE KIDS, BUT **HATE** THE JOB

POSTPARTUM
~~DESPAIR~~ *happiness*

WHAT TO DO WHEN YOU **LOVE** THE KIDS, BUT **HATE** THE JOB

MARISSA ZWETOW, LMFT
contributions from Shoshana S. Bennett, Ph.D.

POSTPARTUM *happiness*

POSTPARTUM *happiness*

www.postpartumhappiness.com

Editing by Kelly Epperson

Cover design by Margaret Cogswell
www.margaretcogswell.com

THANK YOU MOM *for playing such a huge part in contributing to this book. You were my first set of editing eyes, available to brainstorm ideas with me, and you just knew how to fill in the holes. Though your experience of being a mother was very different than mine you understand the importance of my message. I can't thank you enough for helping me make this book a reality.*

THANK YOU SHOSH *for challenging me to see more clearly what I was experiencing, validating me, and then jumping on board and collaborating with me! It was so much fun to work with you.*

NOTE FROM THE AUTHOR

This small but powerful narration of my journey as a new mother gives voice to a topic that is very taboo: I love my child, but I do NOT love the job of being a parent.

This issue, and this book, is not just about postpartum depression. This "feeling" of "I don't like mothering" is not always something that goes away in a few weeks or months. But it IS something you can learn to accept AND you can learn to accept yourself -- and love yourself and your life again.

I want to let other mothers who feel the way I did know that they are not alone; that it is possible to be confident and happy with your role as a mother even if you don't enjoy the actual job of parenting. It is 100% okay to have other passions besides your children.

When my daughter was born, I found myself hating being a mom. This experience was not at all what I expected, and I felt so lost and alone. I wish there had been something written about this topic when I was stuck in shame and embarrassment for feeling this way. I read various books and articles on postpartum depression, but still felt misunderstood.

It wasn't until I was able to love and accept myself fully, even though I did not enjoy the job of taking care of my daughter that I began to find my joy in life again. You can too.

Note from the Author

This book explores beliefs around parenting and how to make positive changes leading to greater happiness for everyone. This text was also written to promote a rational and thoughtful discussion about societal messages and expectations around mothering among professionals and parents. As clinicians we need to see beyond postpartum depression and truly help the woman in front of us.

It is my greatest wish to help ALL mothers feel better.

MARISSA ZWETOW

Marissa Zwetow

PREFACE

"Today my husband asked if I even like being a mom, and I said, 'That is a question I ask myself.'"
- Anonymous Mom

The above quote was not spoken by me, but it could have been. I didn't like being a mom. I loved my daughter, but I didn't love being a mom. My lack of enjoyment for motherhood showed up as postpartum depression. I felt like a failure and a bad mother. Much of my depression was a result of the messages I told myself such as, "You're a bad mother for not being in love with your baby," or "There's something wrong with you if you're not happy caring for your baby."

Based on my research and what I know now, I strongly believe that my depression very well could have been prevented had I been able to connect with other mothers who felt like I did. I would not have felt so alone and so defective. I would still need to learn how to regain my sense of self and happiness, but removing the "what's wrong with me?" question/label would have allowed me to accept my situation with compassion. I could have moved into solution much quicker instead of feeling so stuck and broken.

Postpartum depression to this day is more often defined as a biological illness caused by changes in brain chemistry following birth. There is a significant decline in hormone levels after a mother gives birth to her child and researchers point to that hormonal change as playing a major role in postpartum depression. Why then isn't every woman who gives birth afflicted by postpartum depression? Why do men who clearly do not have hormone changes also report postpartum depression? Or parents who adopt?

I'm not saying brain chemistry or hormones don't play a part in postpartum disorders. Rather, I'm saying the lack of enjoyment of parenting can be a very strong contributor to postpartum depression, not the other way around.

In the beginning I felt no joy in the role of parent and I had nowhere to turn for validation and support.

I was unable to find any explanations of postpartum depression that pointed to lack of enjoyment for motherhood as a cause. I don't mean just the usual stresses of new motherhood such as constant diaper changes and crying and interrupted sleep. I mean so much more than that. Books on postpartum depression do not address this issue.

The messages we receive via society do not give any comfort. At one point I attended a graduate postpartum training with a well-known expert therapist. As she discussed postpartum depression, the absence of satisfaction in motherhood was not posed as one of the causes.

So I point-blank asked her, "What about a mother who just doesn't enjoy being a mother?"

She replied something like: That sounds pathological to me. The same when I hear a woman doesn't want to be a mother. It's unnatural.

Postpartum Happiness

Ouch!

When I heard the word pathological I thought of serial killers. That's not me!

The implication was that there was something innately wrong with me because I am "supposed" to like or enjoy mothering. That's natural, right? That's what you mostly see out in the world. If you don't enjoy being a mother, well, then that is unnatural. That kind of thinking and programming has to stop!

Thank God when I received this comment I was confident and happy, and my depression was behind me. If not, I do believe this therapist with years of experience treating postpartum depression would have confirmed my worst fear, that I was broken not only as a mother, but as a person.

What if I wasn't broken or wrong or sick? What if I just didn't enjoy motherhood? What then? I knew I needed to research this more for myself. These feelings needed to be added as a possible cause for postpartum depression.

If any of this rings true for you, know that you are not alone. Acceptance and self-compassion are the first steps to regaining sense of self. I discovered that hearing from other mothers facing similar struggles who said "me too" was the greatest therapy for me. This assured me that I was not alone and not a monster for feeling this way.

My healing journey from this postpartum experience took much longer than I would have liked, but it led to me where I am today, being able to share with other mothers and clinicians. Not only do mothers need support, the clinicians need to understand that they may have their thinking on postpartum depression backwards.

I did eventually feel confident again and feel like myself, and I knew this phenomenon of not enjoying the role of mother needed to be discussed. I want to assure you that you are not alone. Joy and happiness can be yours. It is indeed possible to love the kids (and yourself) without loving the job of parenting! And there's no shame in that.

"I love my daughter more than anything, but that doesn't mean I have to love being a mom."
- Anonymous Mom

A note to my dear reader –

These "Mom" quotes sprinkled throughout the book are not from me, but they are all real and resonate with me – I could have said them and probably did at one point. These words are what I needed to hear most when I was depressed. To know that other mothers faced a similar struggle was very comforting. The quotes are obtained from various sources. These are real words from real mothers. Perhaps you see yourself in their words too.

TABLE OF CONTENTS

MY STORY

In many ways, I was a typical mother-to-be. My husband and I had married in our thirties, (me, 33; him, 34), and we had wanted and planned for our baby. I loved my career as a mental health therapist and planned to continue working after I gave birth. It also crossed my mind that I may want to stay home with the baby (because I would love it) and that we would be able to manage financially. Either way, I just saw that life would be great. I could not have foreseen how my life would change.

We started trying for a baby shortly after our one-year wedding anniversary. After four months I got pregnant, but miscarried very early on after conception. Doctors assured me this was normal. I dealt with the loss well, allowing for my grief and disappointment, but trusting that God had it all handled. After another five months of trying, I got pregnant again. The pregnancy was viable, and I was healthy. I continued to progress and do all the normal planning, the birth classes, the baby room preparation, and the baby shower. I never doubted that I would be a good mother and that I would absolutely love it.

The pregnancy continued to go well until I was diagnosed with cholestasis at 36 weeks. This is a pregnancy disorder in which the liver starts to react negatively to all the extra hormones and releases bile acids into the blood stream, which is not normal. In general, this is not dangerous for the mother or baby, but induction around 37 weeks is highly recommended. This was devastating to me. I was planning on a natural birth with no drugs. An induction was not part of this plan. I had ten days to prepare myself and to learn more about this new birth plan. I tried to implement any kind of control I still felt I had. Being induced just plain sucked. I was not ready. I did not want it and I am convinced my baby was not ready either.

There is nothing about my daughter's birth that stands out as abnormal or traumatic. She was born vaginally and was healthy, yet for me the event just wasn't what I thought or hoped it would be. I felt somewhat scarred from the whole experience. As soon as my daughter was born she was placed on my chest for what was termed "the golden hour," only there was nothing golden about it for me.

My daughter screamed on my chest for the entire hour. This was somewhat startling and the beginning of realizing the many myths of motherhood I had fallen victim to. As she wailed and cried on my chest, I felt nothing. There was not that instant bond that I had heard about. Why wasn't I in love instantly?

That scream stayed with her for at least a good solid year. It was a scream you could hear across a football field. Everyone commented on it; family, other parents, and our pediatrician (who had been practicing for over 30 years), as if it was unlike any other baby they had heard before. That made my whole new adventure of being a new mom that much more unenjoyable.

Also, I felt a lot of anxiety around breastfeeding. I struggled with getting Cora to latch correctly and my nipples had begun to bleed as a result. It was so painful. As if this wasn't bad enough, I soon learned that she was not getting enough milk and was not gaining enough weight. I sought out several lactation consultants for help and even rented a baby scale.

Every nursing session started with my newborn infant being weighed and then weighed again after nursing and all of this was documented. It may not seem like that big of a deal, but it made breastfeeding miserable. It was a feat and it was measured, graded, and scored. There was nothing natural, peaceful, or relaxing about it. Yet again another myth busted - breastfeeding was not natural, easy, and enjoyable for me.

I had to begin supplementing with formula. This was so incredibly sad for me. After all, breast is best, right? This had also been part of my birth and aftercare plan. I would breastfeed and I would love it. The struggle to breastfeed continued for several months. I was still watching videos and tutorials on breastfeeding six weeks in and wondering why I was not getting this by now.

I had heard that babies have different cries for being hungry, wet, or in pain, etc., but my daughter had one cry and that was her infamous scream. We later learned that she had acid reflux, which translated into a crying, screaming, fussy baby.

Of course, I had no ill will towards my child and never wanted harm to come her way, however I was experiencing regret and if I could have gone back in time I may have undone it all. I didn't like the whole thing; all of it, motherhood and my baby. I didn't understand how I could feel this way about something that was supposed to be this amazing life event. I wanted all of it to go away. The anxiety and insecurities I felt about breastfeeding and wanting everything to go well, along with my lack of enjoyment quickly turned into despair. I felt like such a loser and failure with no hope in sight. Depression was inevitable.

At my 6 week postpartum OB/GYN appointment I was a mess. I was severely depressed and on edge. I was given a postpartum depression screening questionnaire and lied my ass off. I'm not sure if it was due to my embarrassment of how I was experiencing motherhood or my belief that as an experienced licensed therapist I could fix myself or a combination of both. I had no interest in talking about what I was feeling with a stranger, my doctor's physician assistant. I wanted to believe that what I was feeling would pass and that I was just having a difficult transition.

I didn't want to come to terms with the idea of having postpartum depression. I also remember thinking "I'm not depressed, I just don't like this."

The distinction I now know and what led me to write this book is that postpartum depression is caused by a variety of reasons. What is most known and accepted among professionals is that the lack of enjoyment with mothering is a symptom of postpartum depression. Although this can be true, the lack of enjoyment can also be a cause of postpartum depression. This fact can be difficult to accept. As one mother said, "I feel like people flat out lie because it's taboo for women to admit how they feel, like you'll need to turn in your "woman card" or something."

Four years later, I am truly happy now and have a strong bond with my daughter, but I still struggle to find pleasure in parenting. I feel passionate about understanding this phenomenon and accepting it as a norm. It is my belief that not liking parenting is linked to postpartum depression and that the approach to "fix" it is inaccurate and misunderstood. I also believe that this particular cause of postpartum depression can be treated and/or prevented with a better clinical understanding, supportive societal messages, and other mothers saying "me too."

If you're in this boat, know that you will not sink. You and I are not pathological or broken as was suggested to me by that therapist "expert." I love my daughter. I just don't enjoy the job of taking care of her. And there is nothing wrong with that.

PART I: THE JOB SUCKS!

> *"I am disappointed that more people aren't honest about their experiences and that the culture in general perpetuates the myth that motherhood is all-fulfilling. In many ways it flat-out sucks."*
> *- Anonymous Mom*

Having a baby was supposed to add to my life, pure and simple. I envisioned it as the next step after marriage and figured I would love my baby and motherhood. My husband and I were healthy, capable and a normal couple who wanted a baby. I had seen all the baby product commercials implying that being a mother was wonderful. All the movies depict picture-perfect birth scenes and I made note that a bond would happen instantly with my baby. That never happened and the wonderful life I had before was suddenly taken away from me.

Mothers not enjoying parenting? I had never heard about such a thing. I found myself hating being a mother and felt like a monster for feeling this way. I found no empathy or validation that these feelings were normal or acceptable. It was horrible

7

to feel so alone and so ashamed.

There are certain personality types, personal values and past experiences that can cause new mothers to feel out of control and defeated with a new baby. I didn't realize this at the time, but my past successes and achievements, thriving on always finding a way to be on top of my game, would work against me. There was a false sense of control that just because I had wanted it and prepared for it (natural child birth, successful breastfeeding, bonding time with baby, soothing the baby easily, predictable napping and eating schedules, etc.), I could achieve it, the same way I had studied for a test and got an 'A' or reduced my calories and lost weight. Having a baby hit me hard in the face with the realization that I had no control no matter how hard I worked.

"I confessed to my husband one night that I felt we had ruined our lives."
- Anonymous Mom

IT STARTED WITH THE BIRTH

I had planned for and wanted a natural childbirth, so I took the Bradley method classes. Again, this was a false sense of control believing that I could prepare for the childbirth experience I wanted like so many other classes I had taken to achieve something I wanted in life.

The first indication that I would not be delivering the way I had planned was being diagnosed with cholestasis, a condition in pregnancy affecting the mother's liver. I was told I would need to be induced at 37 weeks to ensure the safety of the baby. My birth plan did not include being induced and using Pitocin (synthetic version of oxytocin) which interferes with the body's natural way of inducing labor on its own. This was the first of many disappointments I would experience in the birth of my baby.

I remember the items on my birth plan being eliminated one by one, all the way down to the last item on my list when the doctor cut the umbilical cord which was around my daughter's neck rather than having it pulsate for one minute as recommended by the Bradley Method. I'm not mad at the doctor for making that call to cut the umbilical cord any more than I am mad at my daughter for ruining our "golden hour," the first hour after birth by screaming the entire time. I'm just disappointed that so many things went wrong. These were moments and experiences that were "supposed" to be wonderful and special. Having my childbirth experience go so differently was so sad for me, but there wasn't really time to grieve this because I was on to the next set of disappointments. It was beyond overwhelming, all that went wrong, and this was only the beginning. There were so many incongruities between what I wanted and what it ended up being.

I'M NOT IN LOVE

"I felt like I was taking care of a stranger's child."
- Anonymous Mom

The Job Sucks!

I had seen it over and over again in the movies and television: that instant love, the tears of joy, the touching and holding, the baby gripping onto your finger for the first time. I did not feel that instant love for my baby the second she was placed on my chest. Although there are many mothers just like me who do not feel love for their baby instantly, I just wished I could understand why. The research out there currently doesn't explain why this instant love doesn't happen for every mother, but the information available does normalize that not all mothers feel love immediately for their baby. In this case I knew I wasn't alone, but I still felt like there was something wrong with me.

> *"Everyone talks about how you feel this rush*
> *of love when your newborn is placed on your chest*
> *for the first time. Didn't feel that at all, just*
> *exhausted and terrified."*
> *- Anonymous Mom*

When my baby was placed on my chest after birth I began to feel anxious because of her penetrating scream that lasted the entire hour she was on me. I do feel this infamous scream was a major factor in my not feeling close to her right away. I've talked with many mothers since the birth of my daughter with their own version of their story. Back when I needed to hear it most, a co-worker's response when I asked her about her bond with her baby gave me some comfort. She also struggled with a screaming baby and said "How could anyone bond with that?!" I took that to mean why would anyone be able to feel loving toward a screaming baby. This was reassuring that

I was not abnormal.

My mother had shared with me that caring for me and my brother when we were babies was the hardest time of her life but also the happiest. I couldn't relate at all. Well, at least not to the happy part. Perhaps having closeness with your baby is what is "supposed" to happen because the job of motherhood is incredibly difficult and without that closeness it just plain sucks. How does that expression go? "The hardest job you'll ever love." But for me it was the hardest job and I hated it. Doing this job day in and day out, not having closeness with my baby and feeling so ashamed was a perfect recipe for depression. I've been told that depression can be caused by not saying or doing what you want. Every day I was living a life I didn't want, caring for a baby I was not close with.

But I gave it my best. My mother often commented that I was a great mother. This doesn't surprise me because I did everything that was required of me; going through the motions of caring for my daughter's every need, but it was more out of duty and obligation. I was stuck and had no reference point of how to do it any other way. I longed for emotional support and permission to say this job sucks!

The bond and love did eventually come and has only gotten stronger and stronger. However, no matter how much I love my daughter or how close I am to her, I still cannot say that I love parenting. I'm guessing I still would have said the job sucks even if I had felt immediate closeness with my daughter, but feeling a bond from the beginning sure would have helped.

BABY BLISS LIES

Lie #1 – Breastfeeding will be easy and enjoyable
Breastfeeding was anything but easy and enjoyable. It was

a feat! Effort with no reward! It started with latching issues resulting in bleeding and cracked nipples. Then it turned into lack of milk production resulting in heartache, a sense of personal failure, and formula supplementation.

"I remember my Google searches from that time: When do newborns get easier? Why does my baby cry so much? How do I pump while holding a screaming baby? Will I ever enjoy being a mother?"
- Anonymous Mom

The lie I told myself is that I will have no problem breastfeeding and it will be a relaxing and bonding time with my baby. I put so much pressure on myself to breastfeed. I was educated on the many benefits my own milk had to offer and this benefit to my baby was worth my effort, burden and struggle. When I didn't produce enough milk I turned to lactation consultants who helped with ways to increase my milk supply such as herbal supplements, a rigorous breastfeeding schedule and a change in my diet. I would breastfeed every 3 hours, even at night, waking up my baby to breastfeed rather than allowing her (and myself) to sleep.

I rented a baby scale so I would know just how many ounces I was producing or rather, wasn't producing. I felt such an attachment to the results of this; elation when the scale showed a good amount of milk and disappointment when the number of ounces of milk came in below what was needed for proper nourishment. I would then supplement with formula. Formula with ingredients like high fructose corn syrup (the last thing I wanted to give my newborn) and ingredients I couldn't even pronounce. I was so sad about this. I felt robbed of the wonderful breastfeeding experience I had anticipated when I was pregnant. I was blindsided by how hard this was and the fact that I wasn't producing enough milk for my baby.

I was so consumed with my milk production and proper latching methods that I have no memory of ever being relaxed and just enjoying that time with her. I remember towards the end only breastfeeding her in the morning and then pumping throughout the day. I can't even remember why I did this. Maybe it was easiest at that point, but I do recall pumping and then rocking her with my foot in her carrier. I find this interesting because I thought the effort I gave to pumping a small amount of breastmilk was more important than holding her or interacting with her in any way.

There is now a movement to educate mothers that although breastfeeding does have benefits, it shouldn't be at the expense of the mother's emotional health. We need to let go of the notion that breast is best. The slogan I am most familiar with is 'fed is best.' It is my mission to offer support and education to mothers no matter how they choose to feed their baby.

I finally let go of breastfeeding at 4 ½ months when I was producing about 25% of what my baby needed and other than a morning breastfeeding it was all done by a breast pump. I wish I could say letting this go was a huge relief but it was just one more disappointment behind me with many more to come.

Lie #2 – There will be plenty of soothing, quiet, and peaceful bonding experiences

When I was pregnant, I fantasized about how my mother/baby experience was going to be. Seeing a poster in my doctor's office about the importance of skin-to-skin contact and the benefits to the baby of a mother holding her baby against her bare chest, I knew instantly that this would be me and my baby while we were home together. We would have skin-to-skin contact and it would be dreamy and great.

"I thought motherhood was snuggles and kisses."
- Anonymous Mom

Then reality appeared. This nirvana never happened! I could have allowed her to rest on my bare chest in between her screaming and/or needing something from me, but any time my baby was sleeping or calm without me, it was a much needed break for me and the last thing I wanted was to attach her to me again. The statement that there would be plenty of time for this type of quiet contact and it would be soothing for us both was a lie. My fantasy of snuggle time was just that – a fantasy that never came to be.

"Being a mom has turned out so differently
from what I was expecting."
- Anonymous Mom

Lie #3 – It will be so much fun dressing my baby in all of her cute baby clothes

Being pregnant and planning for my new baby was so much fun for me. As soon as I found out we were having a girl, I began buying clothes for her in anticipation. Everything was so cute! I was excited to dress up my baby the same way I had dressed my dolls when I was younger. These are the joys of having a baby, right? This would be fun for me and would allow me some return on my investment, so to speak. What my daughter actually ended up wearing was a lot of onesies or very simple easy on- easy off clothes which did not include a single one of those cute dresses I had purchased for her. Besides the realities of changing diapers, my daughter also spit up constantly. I mean constantly! She had acid reflux though I don't know if this was the entire reason. She spit up so much that even if I mustered up some effort to get her into one of those darling outfits it was covered by a giant bib to wipe and catch all the spit up. I carried around baby wash cloths like they were going out of style. My husband and I had carpet stain remover ready to go and went through several bottles.

"I felt like I got nothing in return to basically being a slave to this tiny creature."
- Anonymous Mom

Though this is not by far the worst thing a parent can endure, it was still very disappointing for me not to have the baby experience I wanted and planned for. This was yet again one more misrepresentation of how life would be as a mother.

Lie #4 – I'll be able to sleep when the baby sleeps
I understood that caring for a baby would come with sleep challenges, midnight and 3am feedings, however I told myself

it was all going to be worth it. I am one of those people who needs a good night's rest or I am useless the next day. I am also one of those people who can nap well and can do it regularly when I need to.

"I thought I would automatically love being a mom. But I don't. I don't like my entire life being dictated by a toddler."
- Anonymous Mom

I was told to nap when the baby naps and figured this would be no problem for me. What I did not plan for was how unpredictable her naps would be, sometimes napping for 20 minutes, sometimes two hours. That's a big difference in time and that unpredictability made it hard to plan things, including a good solid nap for yours truly. I was often exhausted from lack of sleep the night before and from trying so hard to sleep while my daughter was sleeping. The pressure was on and the clock was ticking.

My thought process went something like this as I lay there trying to sleep: "What if she only sleeps twenty minutes? Oh, ten minutes has now passed already. I only have ten minutes left to sleep. I better fall asleep! But it will only be ten minutes. What good is ten minutes?" Or "Okay, twenty minutes has now passed, so I am now on borrowed time and she might wake up any minute." This led to some pretty exhausting days. Trying to force yourself to sleep can keep you on edge as much as not having enough sleep. It was a wild roller coaster ride.

Lie #5 – my baby will love car rides, stroller rides and baths

"Being a mom has turned out so differently from what I was expecting. Part of that has been because things that I thought every kid liked, my son did not. Taking a bath? Hated it. Going to the park? Cried. Hated the car seat (always did!)."
- Anonymous Mom

My baby didn't like car rides, stroller rides and baths and I was truly shocked. These events were supposed to be calming. I thought warm water and movement would soothe her. Maybe it just depends on the stage of development or differences in baby personalities, but the cure-all tricks of other parents like purposefully putting their crying baby in the car to soothe or induce sleep did not work for us. When my daughter was subjected to car rides, stroller rides and baths, she often screamed her notorious scream and this phase lasted for quite some time.

I felt such anxiety with her screaming in these situations because the task at hand needed to happen. I couldn't not give her a bath. And there were times when she had to be in the car. Whether it was bathing her or driving from point A to point B, I felt like I couldn't escape her screams. I felt like I was carrying around a ticking time bomb. Going on a walk with her in the stroller could start out great with a happy baby passenger then end up with me running as fast I could to get my screaming baby home. Car rides too often turned out the same way. It was maddening.

Lie #6 – I'll love being a mother and won't miss my old life

> *"I had a baby to add to my life, not take away."*
> *- Marissa Zwetow*

I couldn't have predicted how much I would look back and miss my old life. I yearned for the freedom I had to wake up on a Saturday morning after sleeping in a bit, sipping a hot cup of coffee and enjoying a quiet morning while my husband usually slept in longer. I loved the weekends and used to look forward to them. My husband and I would do fun stuff like dine out, hang out with friends, or have a lazy Sunday enjoying some adult beverages at our favorite restaurant patio. This was the life! I was truly happy with it all.

Weekends now looked much different. When I was still breastfeeding, in addition to middle of the night feedings I would be up around 6:00am for another feeding and to start my day. Caffeine was not allowed because of breastfeeding so a hot cup of coffee was out. Instead of relaxing while waiting for my husband to wake up I was now consumed with caring for an infant which probably included a few diaper changes, rocking, bouncing or some sort of soothing and another feeding. My husband would wake up around 9:00am, 3 hours after I had already been up and had conquered half the day. I remember the resentment I felt for him as he stumbled down the stairs after what I assumed to be a pretty leisure wake up.

The rest of the day would have to be worked around my baby's naps which started at three naps a day, then dropped to two naps at six months and finally only one nap at eighteen months. What did it matter though? Where were we going to go anyway? We did do our best to get out of the house with the baby however it always felt like more trouble than it was worth. Having this baby was taking away from my life not adding to it. I grieved the loss of my freedom, my relationship with my husband and most of all my happiness. I wanted it all back!

Whose Job Is It?

> *"I resented him for how much my life had turned upside down and his seem to just carry on."*
> *- Marissa Zwetow*

With depression, exhaustion and just plain misery oozing out of me, my husband became the enemy in my eyes. I resented him for how much my life had turned upside down and his seemed to just carry on. His sleep wasn't disturbed the same way mine was, his career wasn't put on hold, he wasn't a slave to this baby the way I was. I knew my life would be different and I knew that caring for an infant came with challenges. I wasn't shocked by my daughter's cries of hunger at 3 am and I was actually looking forward to taking three months off of work. The problem was that I wasn't happy with being a mother and wanted so badly to blame him for not being in the trenches with me. No matter how much he helped in my mind it was never enough and I felt like he would never be able to understand the hell I was going through.

The Job Sucks!

I never considered myself a feminist, but this whole parenting experience made me so aware (and angry) at the gender role differences placed onto women and men. I even had a hard time with baby shower parties being just for women. Why is it that only women are supposed to have an interest in all things babies? I guess the truth is I was embarrassed that I don't fit the mold when it comes to the traditional female or mother role. I am the mother daring to say I don't enjoy it. I am the mother who works not because of financial reasons but because I find more reward and value in my career than staying home and raising my daughter. My list of how I don't fit the traditional mother role is long.

My inner thoughts swirled around in my head from "What's wrong with me?" to "My husband is a misogynist for expecting me to do everything!" to "Is that stay at home mother of five young children really happy?" to "What society expects of me as a woman and mother is so unfair" and these thoughts always seemed to swirl back to "What's wrong with me that I don't enjoy being a mother?"

Once our daughter was born, my husband and I fell into stereotypical gender roles. In the beginning a lot of the responsibilities that fell on me just made sense since I was breastfeeding and had arranged for three months maternity leave. After three months I returned to work and shortly after that stopped breastfeeding. My husband and I should have been on equal terms then, but the immense burden of caring for our daughter fell on my shoulders.

If my daughter was sick, I was the first option to stay home with her; if there were appointments, I adjusted my work schedule to take her; and if there were any spills, accidents, or messes, I cleaned them up. If my daughter had a runny nose, I was usually the one to wipe it; if my daughter was hungry, I fed her; and if there was a dirty diaper, I felt I always needed to change it. I was often the one on duty and though my husband was right there beside me, I had to ask for his "help." I now know why fathers often refer to being on duty as "babysitting." They identify more with being the help than being the caregiver.

I realize I played a part in this because I made a choice to do everything but I also see that I had fallen victim to gender role expectations of mothers. The other problem is that I really believed I would love being a mother, thus it never occurred to me to divide up the responsibilities the same way we might have if we had adopted a dog.

I found myself in a vicious cycle of doing everything and resenting my husband as I did it. The more I did everything myself, the more I rationalized that I could do it faster and better. I found myself envious of his role as a Father.

I stumbled upon a book with this title translated from German and it gave me great comfort: The Mother Happiness Lie: Regretting Motherhood - Why I'd rather be a father. The author, Sarah Fischer, states "Women who become mothers are forced into the mother role whereas men are still bankers, carpenters, doctors. Everything remains the same [for men.]"

I can relate to Sarah Fischer's book title and wonder if I would have been happier as a father instead of a mother, experiencing all the joys of having kids without all the burden and responsibility of caring for them.

Update: What I know today!

Today the help and support I get from my husband is amazing. I now know that in the beginning I was not very receptive of my husbands' help because it was not the way I would have done it. I wanted to control how he parented, which I imagine left him frustrated and not wanting to help at all. Sadly, I wasn't connecting the dots in how I was playing a part in this vicious cycle.

Today when I need help getting my daughter dressed and out the door I don't worry about the "mismatched" outfit my husband picks or that he doesn't fix her hair the way I would do it. If I need him to fix her a meal I don't worry what's being served (white processed pancakes and syrup.) If I ask him for help washing the dishes I let go of how long the dishes sat in the sink before he got started. I instead look at the outcome; my daughter dressed and ready to go, clean dishes, a child with a full belly and a happy mom.

Sure, sometimes his idea of how to coordinate her outfit or what to feed her leaves me rolling my eyes, but there are also times that he comes up with some great ideas. I remember struggling with my daughters picky eating and feeling at wits end. My husband was taking care of her one afternoon and made her a peanut butter sandwich on whole wheat bread and she loved it. Had I controlled the situation by pre-making her lunch or telling him what to serve her (because only I know what she'll eat), this healthy food choice probably wouldn't have entered into the equation. I am pleasantly surprised time and time again with what a great help he is when I stop controlling him and let go of the belief that I know best because I'm the mom.

I also found myself experimenting with doing less or doing nothing at all. I didn't have a conversation about it, or ask for "help," just simply stopped doing. What would happen if I didn't make my daughter lunch or help her in the bathroom the split second she says "I'm done" with both parents being available? I began to take ownership that I was the one doing a lot of the parenting out of fear of something bad happening if I didn't.

I had resented my husband for not picking up cues the way I did or respond to my daughter's needs at the rate I did, but when I stopped resenting and took ownership for my part and stepped down, he stepped up. This was a simple task, but not always an easy one. I found myself having to sit on my hands to prevent my jumping in, zipping my lips to prevent my telling him how to do it, or sometimes just leaving the room. He may not serve lunch until 3:00pm or it may take my daughter saying "I'm done" 3 times before he helps her in the bathroom, but it did get done. I found this happening more and more by simply realizing that with my husband right beside me I didn't have to jump up the second a parenting task was needed.

My Identity Crisis

"I've always wanted to be a mom for as long as I can remember, but once I became a mom I was like, 'Maybe this is just not for me.'"
- Anonymous Mom

Amidst hating the job of parenting and thinking I was the scum of the earth for feeling this way, I was also devastated that my role as a mother didn't match up to my strong expectations of motherhood that began in childhood when playing with my dolls. I never questioned becoming a mother or doubted that I would have any other feelings other than love and joy. Looking back there was a red flag: I hated babysitting the few times I did it. However, I assumed it would be different when I was caring for my own child. I was a loving person and no one, not even myself, could have or would have deterred me from moving forward with starting a family.

I was thirty-six when my daughter was born. That was a lot of years of dreaming and fantasizing about how this journey of motherhood would go. Before my daughter was born, I had it planned out that because of my age and because I knew I wanted two or three kids, I would try and have babies back to back, like taking extra college courses to graduate sooner. No problem. It will be fine, I told myself. I've got this. Boy, was I wrong.

My husband still wants another child. I'm just not sure I could endure it all again. I completely understand that I could have a totally different experience but then again it could be exactly the same. The sadness I feel about not wanting another child isn't just about letting my husband down but it's also a letdown for me. My ideal white picket fence life included more than one child. But the fact is I thought I would love being a mother and I don't.

Maybe you have felt the identity crisis too. Perhaps you have a longer list of "baby bliss lies" that you have discovered. By now at least you can see that you are not alone. You are not defective. You can love your child and still maintain that the job sucks. But there is hope! You can enjoy being a mother your way!

PART 2: ENJOY BEING A MOTHER YOUR WAY!

"I seem to be more willing to separate from my daughter than my friends. I have friends that never go out and would never work as much as I do but I need to. My daughter is happy to go to school or over to my family. I might not be the perfect mom but I think we have a system that works for us."
- Anonymous Mom

In the beginning, I got caught up in what a "good" mother does. She plays nursery rhyme music in the car for her baby to listen to; she takes her baby to classes to help her development; she talks, sings and teaches her baby at every opportunity, and she enjoys every moment of being a mother.

Well, it turns out I don't enjoy listening to nursery rhymes in the car, I didn't enjoy the classes and I didn't like feeling the pressure of having to spend every moment of my day entertaining or teaching my baby. Participating in these activities that I only did out of guilt or obligation only heightened my lack of enjoyment of being a mother.

Enjoy Being a Mother Your Way!

It took hearing from therapists, mentors, other moms and my own intuition for me to finally get that it was OK to be a mother my way. I realized that my happiness not only mattered but was actually more valuable for my child than participating in activities I didn't want to be doing.

"I don't stress too much about whether my daughter is eating organic or 100% healthy food. She will survive eating Cheerios and cookies sometimes."
- Anonymous Mom

In the past I would compare my way of parenting with other mothers and feel at odds with them or perceive it as "me versus them." Today, I recognize that there is simply a large continuum on levels of involvement and enjoyment when it comes to parenting.

One mother shared with me about playing with her son: "I'm following my son around on the playground, swinging with him, crawling through tubes... I see other moms give me funny looks from the benches and tables nearby. For a second I feel silly, but then my son laughs at me hanging from monkey bars."

This particular mother would place herself high on the continuum of enjoyment in active play at the park with her son, while I would place myself lower because I don't enjoy following my daughter around at the park. Noting differences on the continuum without self-judgement and without the labels "good" or "bad" was valuable to my confidence and enjoyment as a mother. You need to realize and internalize that your way is good for you and your child. If you like to play in the mud with your kid, great. If you don't, great. Don't think another mom is "better" just because she plays more with her child.

The same goes for feeding your child. You know that overall you are providing a healthy lifestyle for your family. If you don't make your own organic baby food or sew your own diapers or whatever trend is popular, do not despair. Take care of your baby your way.

Don't guilt-trip yourself

The list of messages and questions we receive as parents from well-meaning friends and family is pretty long.

- Breast is best
- Motherhood is the best time of your life
- Enjoy this time now because it goes by so fast
- Are they reaching their milestones?
- When are you having another baby?

For a new mother this can be very overwhelming. This can often lead to selling out or in other words doing a lot of things we really don't want to be doing. I found myself doing things out of guilt or pressure. I wanted the best for my baby and didn't realize I could do things a different way, be happy, and still be give the best to my baby.

"When my son was 11 days old, I told the pediatrician that I hated breastfeeding. Her response was to put him on formula because a happy mommy = a happy baby and a happy daddy."
- Anonymous Mom

That pediatrician needs to spread the word. Not all medical professionals would give that advice and they need to.

Enjoy Being a Mother Your Way!

I've stumbled upon more and more articles talking about mothers who made a choice to either stop breastfeeding or never to start. The mothers in these articles spoke about their dislike for breastfeeding for numerous reasons: lack of freedom from always needing to be around to feed their babies; the burden and anxiety of being the sole (or at least main) food source; sore, cracked, bleeding and leaky nipples; and the lack of enjoyment from sitting for hours on end nursing their babies. In the online article titled *Opting out of breastfeeding was the best thing I did*, Jill Simonian writes "I'll make it quick and dirty: The reason I chose to not nurse either of my babies is because I simply did not want to." The mothers in these articles identified what breastfeeding cost them emotionally and made a choice to stop. The message is that sometimes breast is not best. I love the mothers that dared to come forward to share about their decision to stop breastfeeding and how that decision was right for them.

When I work with mothers, I listen to what they really want or don't want. This often requires a lot of work exploring limiting beliefs and clearing out the gunk in their heads (shoulds, guilt, obligation, etc.) One mother felt tremendous guilt for taking time away from her baby to have fun with her friends. Another mother believed that her role as a stay-at-home mother meant she was supposed to do all the cooking and cleaning even though she despised how much time she spent in the kitchen.

Once we cleared away whatever story was playing in their heads about why they needed to continue doing what they didn't want to do or not doing what they wanted to do, a true desire emerged. Then the fun begins when I invite the possibility of that desire becoming a reality no matter how impossible it may seem to them at first. I also propose the idea that a happy mom is worth so much more to her baby than a mother who is burdened with "shoulds" and obligations.

> *"I let my kid watch TV more than I ever thought I would and I'm good with it! I need a break!"*
> *- Anonymous Mom*

Today I self-examine what I want all the time. I remember one evening being tired and just wanting to watch TV. I wanted to watch my shows, not Bubble Guppies or Mickey Mouse Play-house. On this particular evening, I was alone with my 3-year-old daughter while my husband was out of town. I explored the possibility of each of us watching the shows we wanted and came up with a great solution. My daughter watched her shows on her IPad and I watched my shows on the TV. For a good two hours my daughter and I sat side by side on the couch that night watching our shows. I was in heaven, feet kicked up, enjoying my shows and enjoying the company of my daughter. For us this was a definite win-win but I'm certain the list of parenting "rules" that were broken was endless; too much screen time, not enough quality one-on-one time, no child development or learning took place. I could just hear the parenting police saying "This kind of parenting is just plain selfish and neglectful!" We need to rewire the voices of the parenting police.

What I've witnessed and heard from other parenting coaches is that when a parent simply does whatever their child wants to do (and not at all what the parent wants to do), the parent tends to go unconscious or "check out" when playing with their child. In other words, they are not fully present with their child. They're not giving themselves permission to choose how to play with their child. I'm not saying I never participate in an activity that my daughter wants to do or that is needed for her development. Rather I'm saying I give myself permission to make conscious choices about what I want to do. Sometimes this can lead to disappointing my daughter or it can lead to doing an activity just for my daughter. It can also lead to hiring or delegating a task to someone else. Sometimes we compromise; she wants to go the park (which is not my favorite) and I want to play or read on my phone so off we go to the park with my phone in hand.

Honor your truth

Gary Acevedo, MS, creator of the weekend intensive Innovative Parenting & the Miracle of Family, states, "What if the way to be the best parent was to make sure that you honor your truth, giving of your time and self only when it is really true for you? You would end up giving much more of yourself because you are making a choice and not succumbing."

Prior to becoming a parent, I probably would have judged a parent at the park who was on their phone. I would have questioned why they didn't want to play with their child. Now I get why they're on their phone or at least I get why I'm on my phone. The truth is I find more enjoyment in being on my phone than following my child around the park or playing pretend. It's not my thing and when I parent today I get to choose what works best for me. Sometimes I play totally on her terms, but at other times I do my thing, looking up, smiling, and engaging with her every few minutes.

Brene Brown gives a beautiful example in her lecture *The*

Power of Vulnerability: Teachings on Authenticity, Connection and Courage when she talks about judgment from others and how it really shouldn't stop you from being yourself. She gives an example of what appears to be a very well put together or "perfect" family sitting in front of her at church. Brene notes her observations about the family: several children under the age of ten, well dressed in white dresses, well behaved, singing their hymns on cue, etc. She compares them to the Von Trapp family from The Sound of Music. Brene goes on to share that her first observation or judgment is how strange this is and not what you might expect of a family with young children at church. She calls a friend who also observed this family at church and they compare notes. They make judgments about this family saying things like "something's not right" or "how bizarre." Her point is that even this so called "perfect family" will be judged and talked about.

My own takeaway from this story is to do what makes you happy because if you're worried about society's expectations or judgements, guess what? They're always going to judge you no matter what you're doing, whether it's your best or your worst. Why not dare to just do what you want and be happy?

Jim Carrey during his commencement speech in 2014 at Maharishi University of Management shares a great story about the value in doing what you love versus playing it safe (another "should" in life.) He talked about how his father wanted to be a comedian but that he took a "safe" job as an accountant instead of pursuing his love for comedy. Jim Carrey stated how his father ended up losing his "safe job" and the family struggled to get by. He makes the point that "you can fail at doing what you don't want so you might as well take a chance at doing what you love."

These stories remind me that doing what I want and doing

what makes me happy is so important, not just in parenting but in all areas of my life. Though I will admit that doing what I wanted to do as a parent was the most difficult. I felt there were so many more "shoulds" placed on me as a parent than in any other area of my life. The more I made it up that I should be doing what I didn't want to do, the more miserable I got. I was denying myself what I wanted and ultimately my happiness.

Quality versus quantity

> *"Our time together was sweeter when we had*
> *a break from each other."*
> *- Anonymous Mom*

As I mentioned earlier I make conscious choices about how I spend time with my daughter. When I do something that my daughter wants to do and it is not my favorite, I make that choice and participate fully. It's time to let go of what a "good parent" is supposed to do. Honor yourself. As Gary Acevedo says, "Thirty minutes of truly being present with a child is more valuable than three hours of being with them while you are checked out."

According to an article written by Brigid Schulte in the Chicago Tribune March 29, 2015, there is no relationship between how kids turn out (children's academic achievement, behavior and emotional well-being) and the amount of time parents spend with them. In the article, Schulte quotes Melissa Milkie, a sociologist at the University of Toronto, who said "I could literally show you 20 charts, and 19 of them would show no relationship between the amount of parents' time and children's outcomes. . . . Nada. Zippo."

Not only was there no correlation between achievement and time spent but in the same article, Schulte writes about one study noting that parent time can actually be harmful to a child when the parents are stressed, sleep-deprived, guilty and anxious. Schulte writes that according to Kei Nomaguchi, a sociologist at Bowling Green State University, the findings consistently showed that ". . . mothers' distress is related to poor outcomes for their children." These outcomes included behavioral and emotional problems and "even lower math scores."

Consistently doing what I was not enjoying out of obligation and guilt led to depression. It just makes sense that this would also lead to all kinds of developmental complications in my daughter if I had continued on that path. The above article only talked about developmental complications, but I can't help but address more serious issues such as physical or emotional abuse caused by stressed out and anxious parents. I boldly propose that in many cases child abuse can be prevented when a parent honors their own wants and needs before their children's.

"If my oxygen mask isn't on first, we all sink."
- Anonymous Mom

Today I do enjoy spending time with my daughter, but I have so many things in place to help me be a happy mom. My daughter goes to preschool every day and I actually look forward most days to spending time with her in the evenings and weekends. I spend more time doing activities we both like and less time doing only the activities she likes but the difference is my presence and participation in all of them. I wish I had this awareness and knowledge earlier on in the infant and baby stage instead of going through the motions and being "checked out." Now it is about quality time; quality time for me and quality time with my daughter.

Hire or delegate someone else to do it

"Our relationship changed so much for the better when she started a preschool program where she would get that different interaction."
- Anonymous Mom

One of the things I am most proud of is my self-care and overall satisfaction of life. I recognize many aspects of parenting I don't enjoy so I've hired help. A lot of help! For example, my daughter goes to daycare/preschool 9-5 Monday through Friday. Though this is nothing out of the ordinary for working parents, the difference is that I work part time. I don't feel the need to be with her if I'm not working unless I genuinely want to. I take time for myself and it is wonderful! A mother's dream! I get to work-out during the day, take cat naps if I'm tired, schedule lunch with a friend, etc. When I pick up my daughter I am happy to see her and she gets a happy mother in return. I enjoy my daughter so much more because of how

Postpartum Happiness

I have set it up.

In addition to having this time to myself my daughter is learning. She is learning things I would have never thought to teach her or am just not that motivated to do. I remember an early visit with my pediatrician who would always share his thoughts on how to interact, teach and engage with my child. He told me to teach her colors. He said one way to do it is to decide on a color each day and keep that color theme throughout the day. When the color of the day is red, upon waking her up, let her know about the color of the day. Dress her in red clothes and talk to her about the color red. Make or give her red foods that day and again talk about it with her. Point out red things all day long and continue the theme of red. Finish up the day with a story about all the things we did that day involving the color red.

That might be fun for some mothers, but I was exhausted just hearing about his idea. There are many ways to teach children and you can find what is right for you.

In my earlier days of postpartum depression and lacking confidence in my parenting I would have done this activity of teaching my daughter colors and hated every minute of it. I would have fooled myself into thinking I was doing a service to my daughter or fooled myself that she wouldn't know just how "checked out" and miserable I was. There is also a good chance I would have given up on doing this activity and shamed myself for being a bad mother.

Today when I hear a suggestion like this, I nod and smile to keep the peace and think to myself "Not a chance!" This teaching lesson in colors sounds dreadful. It's just not me! Someone else can teach her colors and that is exactly what is happening on a daily basis. I love my daughter's preschool and she loves it too. She interacts with other children, eats different foods, learns so much and gets a happy mother at the end of the day. I also utilize my husband and mother for help; there are activities they enjoy doing with their daughter and granddaughter.

Believing that it is your job or your responsibility to do everything is limiting your enjoyment of life. Also, your kids will benefit because they are getting a happy, energized, loving mom. In this day and age, you can hire someone to do almost anything. If money is a barrier, find it in the budget or be creative and find a student or neighbor or lower cost alternative. Make it happen! It's an investment you will get great returns on.

Carolyn's Success by Dr. Shosh

My colleague and contributor to this book, Dr. Shoshana Bennett, (See Note to Clinicians at the end) shared with me a mom success story regarding a friend of hers: My good friend Carolyn is one of the best examples of how a mom can set up her mothering life so she can most enjoy it. Carolyn's businessman father had taught her long ago how to delegate, and it felt natural to approach every job with this same practical attitude. She arranged mothering the same way she had always done in business. How smart and healthy this was! Carolyn knew she would have disliked much of the mothering job and she wanted to enjoy her daughter.

Her entrepreneur husband was traveling the globe creating businesses, so Carolyn hired a live-in nanny. Carolyn was clear when hiring the nanny that the duties entailed also supporting Mom (Carolyn). The nanny came a month before the baby's due date to set up the nursery. Carolyn already had a housekeeper who had taken care of her during six months of pregnancy bed rest as well as cleaned the house, which she continued to do postpartum. Once the baby was born, the nanny accompanied

Carolyn to all baby-related appointments, did much of the family shopping and cooking, and also joined them on outings. The nanny was often on duty at night, bringing the baby to Carolyn to nurse, then doing all necessary baby tasks that followed. After returning to work, the nanny brought the baby to Carolyn's office to nurse. Carolyn had no negative stories spinning in her mind about any of this. Quite the contrary, it simply made sense to her. There was zero guilt or shame. She thought, why would she make herself do jobs at which others were better and she also didn't like? After all, she'd never do that in any other job when she was in charge!

From the moment her daughter was born, Carolyn adored her, and to this day they've always had a wonderful relationship. By hiring others to take care of the tasks at which they were expert, Carolyn freed up her energy to do the things she loved to do with her child.

Carolyn is an excellent example of how a mom can take good care of herself to enjoy motherhood -- which is then best for her child and her marriage. Each of us should design our lives (as much as finances can possibly allow) so that we can enjoy and be the happiest people and therefore the best mothers we can be.

Your passion doesn't have to be your children

> *"I wish I loved it more. I want to be that mom that does crafts and loves to cook meals, but I love my career and I'm good at it. I love my son fiercely. I'm happy with the "type" of mom I am."*
> *- Anonymous Mom*

Enjoy Being a Mother Your Way!

Hearing that my passion didn't have to stem from my child was such a relief. I attended a 5-day "Breakthrough to Success" seminar with Jack Canfield, one of the leading teachers on achieving personal success, when this message hit home for me. Throughout the five days of this event, there were several guest speakers talking on different topics. One of which was Kathleen Seeley (founder and owner of Massively Human LeadershipTM) who took the stage to guide the audience through The Passion Test, a tool to elicit one's passions in life. Kathleen gave instructions to create a list of at least ten items you are passionate about. Such items might include changing or influencing the world, becoming a millionaire, speaking in front of thousands of people or vacationing in Greece.

Kathleen displayed her top 10 passion list for the audience to see and shared that she was actually surprised that spending time with her kids made her list this time around. The list changes and/or can be updated as your passions and interests change. She shared that in her many revisions of her passion list this was the first time her children had made her list. Then said the magical words that I will never forget. "If you are a parent, it's OK if your children don't make your passion list."

It's as if she was speaking directly to me. I heard this and thought "It is?" and "I'm not a bad person if this is the case?" This was incredibly healing to take in because the truth is my daughter was not my passion and this still remained a struggle for me at that time. I love my daughter with all my heart and was beginning to find joy both on my own and through caring for her but parenting her was not my passion at that time and still isn't.

I asked Kathleen how she arrived at knowing her passion did not have to be from her children and that this did not make her less of a mother. She told me about returning back to work after staying home with her third child when the baby was only a few months old, as she was not happy as a stay-at-home mother. Kathleen worked in a male-dominated field and recalled receiving flak from a client who said a mother should be home with her children. This statement affected her negatively at the time because Kathleen was struggling with her own guilt about working. She reached out to her mother for guidance and asked how she had handled being a working mom. Kathleen shared that what was funny was that her mother reminded her that she had actually been home with her until she went to 5th grade and then she returned back to work. All Kathleen had remembered growing up is that her mother worked.

Kathleen realized that even if she chose to stay home out of guilt, there was no guarantee of what her children would even remember or that it even mattered to them as much as she was imagining it did. She knew that the greatest gift she could give her children and to herself was to make mindful decisions about what makes her happy and to act on that.

Every mother needs to take in those words.

"I genuinely enjoy my work. I have a fulfilling career and never allow myself to feel guilty about taking business trips or attending industry events."
- Anonymous Mom

When I returned to work after my maternity leave, it felt so good to be back. At that time, I worked as a group therapist for a drug and alcohol recovery center that focused on healing trauma. As you can imagine the work could be intense, however I really did enjoy it. On one particular day, I took a client through a role play, working to heal some of her past trauma. The client did some deep work and experienced some amazing insights. The look on her face afterwards was that of freedom and self-acceptance. Days like that were not that uncommon but I remember on this day not only feeling passionate about my work but questioning why I felt more alive at work than I could have ever imagined feeling being home and caring for my baby.

I have since met many mothers who get more "reward" from their work than the job of parenting. And that is okay! It is normal and wonderful to love your career. It does not mean that you do not love your child. You can love your child AND love your job. For some that job is parenting. For others it is not.

Being passionate about caring for my daughter or spending time with her may increase throughout different stages of our lives or it may not. I no longer beat myself up about this. My daughter is loved and well taken care of. My daughter gets the privilege of having a happy mom who takes good care of herself and follows her passion. I am proud of this and proud to be spreading this message to my daughter and to other mothers who may be struggling with this internal conflict.

My family! My choice!

Kid-free. One and done. Two and through. The more the merrier. My family! My choice! Why make a statement about it? Well I guess, because for me being one and done was not an easy choice. I felt pressure from my husband, friends and family and society in general telling me one is not enough. "When are you having another baby?" "Your daughter needs a sibling." "It's selfish to only have one." I hoped for some validation on the idea of stopping at one baby when I was reading books on postpartum depression, but I never found it. Instead I was confused and disappointed when the last chapter in the book was on having another baby and how to deal with a possible subsequent battle of postpartum depression the next time. I understand the need for this chapter when the postpartum depression is truly a biological illness, but what about the moms like me that were depressed from the lack of enjoyment and disappointment in what motherhood really turned out to be. There wasn't a chapter addressing and validating what we were experiencing.

The chapter I was hoping for would have included advice on what to do if you feel guilty for not having any more children; what to say to your loved ones when they bring it up; what to do when you feel alone in your struggle not to have any more kids. Had I read this chapter I would have been validated. *See! The experts on the topic didn't think I was selfish. They knew exactly what I was going through and were making a highly educated recommendation for my well-being and happiness.*

So here I am today, one and done, and (for the most part) confident and happy with my choice. I am however sad that I couldn't give my husband another baby and occasionally I worry I may regret not having another child or feel guilty that my daughter lost out from not having a sibling. I am wise enough to know that for today entertaining that self-doubt is not reason enough for me to go another round. I remember reading an article where a struggling mother said that having another baby would mean both children would get half of a mother rather than her only child now getting a whole mother. I could relate so much to that. I know the greatest gift I can give my daughter and husband is a happy mother and wife.

PART 3: ENDING THE SHAME!

My depression had a lot to do with the shame and embarrassment I felt for not enjoying motherhood. If I had been around mothers who felt the same and/or had enlightened physicians, mentors and therapists, my story would have been totally different. They would have let me know that I was normal and perfectly okay for feeling this way. My depression could have been prevented, but let's face it, until now this topic has been taboo and not talked about. The message we get is: "Mothers who don't enjoy parenting are SELFISH!"

The majority of mothers I've encountered both hoped and expected they would be happy and fully enjoy their role as a mother. When this fell short, despair and embarrassment followed. My work with my clients is about ending their shame for feeling this way.

I'm here to send a new message to mothers (and the world): ***A lack of enjoyment in parenting or even a lack of interest in having children is simply a difference in preference.*** It does not mean something went wrong biologically or that you are defective in any way.

Knowing that I was perfectly okay in how I felt solved part of the battle. The other part was letting go of the list of all the things I "should" be doing day in and day out as a mother.

Ending the Shame!

Let me shout it from the rooftops: Letting go of the "should's" and pursuing one's passion (what makes you come alive) is not only NOT selfish but so important and needed in this world.

"Don't ask yourself what the world needs.
Ask yourself what makes you come alive and then
go do that, because what the world needs is
people who have come alive."
- Howard Thurman
Author, Philosopher, Theologian,
Educator, Civil Rights Leader

What's "wrong" with me? I'm different!

For the longest time the song "what's wrong with me? I'm different!" played on in my internal radio station. I knew the melody and every verse. It would start when I would compare myself to other mothers, and would repeat again when some-one would ask me when I was having more children, and got really loud when my own husband would bring up the topic of wanting more kids.

There are so many messages out there of mothers having maternal instincts, a biological time clock for reproducing or nurturing qualities perfect to care for a baby. I joked that I just didn't get the mom gene, but this suggestion implies that something did go wrong in my biological wiring. I can laugh about this but in the end I was hurting myself by implying there was something wrong with me. Today I choose not to engage in this kind of comparing or judging. Instead I choose to celebrate who I am and confidently share what I know to be true with other mothers. I want to end the shame around this taboo subject. If you are a woman who does not enjoy parenting, know that it is NORMAL to feel this way! You are just fine!

What's expected of me?

I've never been a big fan of the idea that not having kids or only having one child is somehow "selfish." I just don't get it. The irony is I had a child for selfish reasons: I wanted one, pure and simple. It was my choice, my decision, my life. So how does that change if a woman chooses to have just one? Or chooses to have none at all? Is someone selfish for only having two children? Who determines if we get that label or not?

Some folks advance the argument for having a minimum of two children because the kids will have then have a playmate or learn valuable life lessons from a sibling. That is not always the case. You can have ten kids and that does not guarantee good relationships or "lessons." A mother who has "too many" children could be deemed selfish as well: "She needs to give her love and attention to those she already has." Who gets to decide what the magic number is?

Many millennials are focusing on other life goals and careers rather than having children. This could be a future trend of generations to come as choosing not to have children becomes more accepted; however, as it still stands today, my generation and past generations often criticize millennials for being "self-absorbed." Again, labels and judging.

According to an article written by Brad Mattes (lifenews. com 2/20/17), he writes, "Millennials are choosing to have pets over children." The article quotes one millennial who stated, "They [pets] give us a greater purpose without making our lives mainly about theirs." Mattes response to her reasoning was: "I was stunned by her self-centered transparency." Why not instead applaud an honest and brave response? I can't help but wonder if there will always be criticism for making a choice that goes against the "norm" -- no matter how much happiness it brings? The new normal needs to be one of letting each mother decide what is best for her life. One kid, two, or twenty, we do not have a right to make anyone feel wrong, defective, or less than.

Today it is my level of happiness that tells me when I'm on track or off track, not how much I conform or fit in. I understand the pushback I may receive at times for choosing my happiness over someone else's ideals, but the consequences for not listening to my happiness compass comes at a great cost to my wellbeing and ultimately the wellbeing of my child. The thing that people seem to forget is that a woman loves her child deeply, even if she does not love the job of parenting.

Event + Response = Outcome (E+R=O)

This formula - Event + Response = Outcome (E+R=O) - created by Dr. Robert Resnick, a psychotherapist, explains how it is our responses and reactions that shape our outcome and not so much the event itself. It is the messages or stories we tell ourselves about the event that ultimately shape the outcome.

The event for me was not enjoying parenting. I didn't get to vote on that feeling, I could only report on it. If I had a choice in the matter I would choose enjoyment every time. Reporting on my feelings is no different than reporting on whether or not I like a certain food. The event was not enjoying parenting: the response to that was something along the lines of, "I'm a bad mother," or "I'm defective," and the outcome was depression and despair.

The response to that same event could have been something

like: "This is perfectly normal and other mothers have encountered this also," or "It's okay to receive help with parenting and focus on other aspects of my life," or "Not enjoying parenting does not mean I'm a bad mother." The outcome could have been very different for me and maybe I wouldn't have fallen into a depression knowing I was not alone and not to blame.

I know I couldn't have prevented all the loss and disappointment I was feeling, but feeling disappointment is much different than blaming myself. I needed to acknowledge my disappointment and my grief over the loss of the fantasy. In fact, it was damn disappointing! I expected to have this amazing bond and motherhood bliss. No one was more surprised and upset than me!

It's common for mothers to turn their disappointment of their mothering experience into self-blame. One mother, "Amber," who came to see me, expressed the disappointment she had in herself for not enjoying being a mother to her newborn and acted as if she had caused it. Amber knew no other answer except that it had to be her fault. She was somehow to blame. I helped Amber see that she was not in control of how she felt any more than someone can control what foods they like or they prefer rock music to opera. I validated the disappointment she felt, but I also helped to change her response from "I'm disappointed in myself" to "I'm so disappointed that that is not what I expected." This new response changed the outcome from despair to hope. Amber needed to feel and acknowledge her grief and disappointment just like I did with the birth of my daughter. Removing her shame and self-loathing was needed in treating her postpartum depression.

Another mother, "Jenny," came to see with a similar experience of being disappointed in herself because her birth experience went so differently than she had planned and imagined.

Ending the Shame!

Jenny had an unplanned C-section which was even harder on her because of all the time and effort she did to prepare for a natural childbirth. Jenny shared with me that she wondered what she could have done differently to prevent the C-section. Jenny even felt bad for feeling bad because after all she had delivered a healthy baby.

The event for Jenny was having a C-section, the response was disappointment in herself, and the outcome was guilt and depression. I challenged this belief and she was able to come to the conclusion that she couldn't have done anything different. I then invited Jenny to fully feel her disappointment that the birth did not go as planned. It was like a light bulb went off when she realized her true disappointment was in the event and that it wasn't about anything she had done wrong. We were able to change Jenny's response to the event and even though the outcome may still have been grief or sadness, this is very different than experiencing shame.

Not only can we change our responses to an event, but we can also change the event in some cases. For example, the event was lack of enjoyment in parenting, the response was I'm a bad mother for feeling this way, and the outcome was despair. The choices and changes I made led to a new event: increased enjoyment in parenting. The new response was self-acceptance and confidence and the new outcome was happiness.

That is the response that more mothers can feel, and that is my mission.

Perspective Is Everything by Dr. Shosh

It is not what happens to us that shapes and affects us, it is our reaction -- our perspective about what happens to us that does. The "stories" we tell ourselves can make all the difference in how we feel about our experiences, our lives, and ourselves. For instance, if a woman in labor hemorrhages, she may or may not become emotionally traumatized depending upon how she processes the experience. Likewise, a divorce or miscarriage doesn't necessarily feel bad and a marriage or new baby necessarily feel good. What each individual mind does with the objective raw experience will determine how a person feels.

It's the messages we tell ourselves that can lead to joy, despair, or anything in between. The job of mothering is rewarding, and quite challenging. Sometimes moms think, "Since I'm not always enjoying taking care of my baby, I must be a bad mom," or "I'm a terrible mother for feeling this way." If a mom believes those thoughts, the outcome can easily be shame, hopelessness, and depression. In other words, it is not the mothering per se that causes the depression. Rather, it is the stories created in the mind that plague and cause the despair.

No one is in control of his or her thoughts or feelings. Thoughts and feelings just pop in. They simply appear. We can only be aware and observe our thoughts and feelings. What can be changed, however, is our perspective about our thoughts and feelings. If the perspective is, "I'm an awful, abnormal woman," that will have a very different effect on us than, "This is a very common and normal feeling!"

Whether the thought or feeling about not enjoying parts of mothering is a temporary symptom of postpartum depression or a more long-term experience, she can give herself a new perspective with statements such as, "I am a good mother regardless of whether I'm always enjoying the job. I love my children very much and they love me. I am learning how to find my joy as a mother and I don't need to fit anybody else's image of what a good mother is!"

Ending the Shame!

The healing power of hearing "me too"

"For me, just hearing other moms say that being a mom sucks sometimes made me feel better."
- Anonymous Mom

The famous singer Adele has spoken openly about having postpartum depression and gave a great example of how hearing from others who feel similarly can affect us positively. According to statements she made in an interview (today.com Oct 31, 2016), Adele said she worried that she made "the worst decision of her life" after she had her son but talking honestly with other mothers about her postpartum depression helped end her feeling of shame. Adele was able to hear from other mothers saying those powerful words "Me too." She was able to attach a different response (I'm not alone) to the event (not enjoying motherhood) and the outcome was that her shame and depression lifted. That is possible for you too!

This book may be brief, but its purpose is huge. Please join me in this mission. Let us be that voice for other mothers daring to speak the truth and to say "me too." There are so many moms out there who need to know that they are not alone in their struggle and that their shame can be lifted. Please read this book and gift one to a mom you know. Tell other mothers that they are okay. Let's reduce the vast numbers of mothers who go through depression. You can love your child without loving the job of being a parent. Let's let go of the labels and judging. Let's all be the best moms we can be, each in our own way.

NOTE TO CLINICIANS BY DR. SHOSH

Throughout the years I've enjoyed wonderful connections and have felt deep satisfaction from helping thousands of moms. During a Postpartum Action Institute workshop, a participant identified herself as having had postpartum depression, but there was an element of her experience that stood out. She attributed much of her struggle with PPD to not enjoying the job of mothering. The way she articulately described eventually bonding with her baby but still not liking the job clicked so loudly I thought everyone in the room heard it.

I asked her, "Are you sure you had postpartum depression?" She was taken aback by my question and exclaimed, "Of course!" But later that day she acknowledged that first, she had never before been asked that question, and second, she had never challenged what had seemed like an obvious assumption. She was realizing that although she had indeed been depressed following the birth of her daughter, there had been something identifiably different about her case that is typically not acknowledged openly by anyone -- including professionals. This lovely and honest truth-telling mother who helped to gel this essential piece in my mind was Marissa Zwetow.

I have authored five books on perinatal mental health, but Marissa's book you hold now is different, and during this collaborative project with her I received an increasing number of flashes of insight and what seemed like lightning bolts of understanding regarding this particular issue.

After three decades of work with depressed new mothers, I finally "downloaded" that missing link -- that piece that I had always known was affecting some mothers, but I hadn't handled it as well as I could have. Now is the time to fix it – to add to our repertoire of supportive statements and concepts we offer the desperate women who contact us. The party line with depressed mothers is to tell them that, as the depression lifts, they will not only feel more bonded with their babies, but they'll love being a mom and taking care of their babies. We tell them that in fact it's the depression suppressing their enjoyment both of their babies and also of the work involved. We tell them with assurance that when they're well, they won't feel so burdened with the work, and their love for their babies will make it all good. In many situations this is exactly what happens – but it's so important not to assume and make it simplistic.

I vividly remember back in the 1980's working with a new mom who clearly loved her baby, but no matter how much reassurance I gave her, she continued to insist that she's re-pelled by the baby care and certain she'd never be okay with it. She felt resigned to it, and that's what was depressing her. In every other area of her life, socially and professionally, she was joyful. She asked me, "But isn't it possible I would have been happier not having a baby?"

I tried so hard to help her feel better that I missed something. I agreed with her that much of the care required for young ones could feel mundane, but I attempted to convince her that after a while she wouldn't mind it. I wasn't able to completely "hear" what she was saying and feeling, and therefore wasn't able to give her all she required. There must be a reason why this mommy and our conversation have continued to stay etched in my mind for decades. It's one of those rare experiences that left me feeling unsettled, as opposed to the usual satisfaction. In retrospect, I imagine it might have been helpful to tell her, "It's ok to love your baby and dislike the work. I understand, and, there's hope. Let's help you figure out how to create a way to enjoy motherhood."

What has been left out of our perinatal mental health trainings to at least some degree is the normalizing of not enjoying what is often accepted as the typical job of mothering. As Marissa states in her story, not enjoying motherhood is often pathologized by professionals; it is not accepted let alone normalized. That piece in depressed and anxious mothers can be very strong and actually cause much, if not all, of the depression and anxiety in some moms. To ignore it is not doing our clients any service.

My sincere wish is that people working with struggling new mothers and those who love them will be able to fully accept the fact that even excellent mothers might not like much of their new job (the way they think they're supposed to do it). Total permission and encouragement will then be given to help them accept these feelings without judgment and best of all to design an individual plan so that they can enjoy what can be an amazing adventure.

The decision to support Marissa's book is an easy one for me. I hope this message reaches parents -- and the professionals who support them.
SHOSHANA S. BENNETT, PH.D.
http://DrShosh.com

A LETTER TO MY DAUGHTER

Dear Cora,

I am writing you this letter so that you will always know how much you are loved and wanted, despite my candid honesty about not enjoying the actual job of parenting. A lot of my dissatisfaction came from my own faulty thinking. I allowed guilt to guide me, not knowing how or when to ask for help, and ultimately I believed there must be something wrong with me. It led me on quite a journey which resulted in this book. My determination to find an answer will have a positive impact on mothers who struggle with the job of parenting. No longer will they have to endure shame, guilt and depression the way I did.

This book has many wonderful principles that I promise to pass on to you - principles such as accepting yourself no matter how different you are, questioning beliefs that limit you, and doing what makes you happy despite the opposition.

My dearest daughter, I'll always be there to support you in pursuing your dreams no matter what they may look like! I love you!

Love,
Mom

GET SUPPORT!

1 in 7 new mothers will experience a postpartum mood disorder, so know you are not alone and know that your depression may simply be because of the event and day to day life of being a mom not "living up to the hype."

Transitioning from pregnancy to motherhood is not easy and often doesn't fit your pictures of what you thought it would be or what you wanted it to be. This gap between what you hoped and how it actually is can leave you feeling devastated and confused. You know you should reach out for help or support, but the embarrassment stops you.

Are you tired of pretending that everything is great and you're "so happy" being a mother? If you were hoping it would get better with time, but it's not and now it's affecting your marriage and relationships, you are not alone.

A lot of mothers struggle and don't talk about it due to embarrassment and shame. It doesn't have to be this way. You can feel joy about yourself, your baby, and your relationships. You can find yourself again.

I can help because I understand what you're going through. As you just read, I struggled with postpartum depression and understand the sadness, the isolation, and the feeling of being blindsided by its hold on you. My mission is to help mothers struggling with any type of postpartum adjustment.

Please reach out. Let me share my wisdom, strength, and hope. It can get better.

You don't have to go it alone. Text me now at 949-424-3034 or e-mail me at info@postpartumhappiness.com. Find me at www.postpartumhappiness.com where you can find your joy again!

ABOUT THE AUTHOR

Marissa Zwetow, a licensed marriage and family therapist, is founder and owner of Postpartum Happiness where she helps mothers who struggle with their roles, responsibilities and enjoyment of motherhood.

Marissa lives in Orange County, CA with her loving and supportive husband, Tony, and her one-and-only-child by choice, Cora. Marissa understands all too well the shame, guilt and disappointment that come when motherhood is not what was expected. She knew there was more to her journey than just postpartum depression and had to write about it in hopes of helping other mothers who struggle like she did.

Marissa offers individual therapy in person, phone or video call, as well as relationship coaching to learn valuable and proven skills to restore intimacy in your marriage. Get more information at www.postpartumhappiness.com or reach out directly to info@postpartumhappiness.com.

Find your joy again!

Made in the USA
San Bernardino, CA
26 October 2018